TEA TIME
COLORING BOOK

Marty Noble

Dover Publications, Inc.
Mineola, New York

A delightful array of images evoking the elegant custom of tea time awaits you in this unique coloring book. Set against intricately patterned backgrounds and brimming with beautifully detailed serving dishes and cutlery, tablecloths and doilies, curtains, and other evocative tea time motifs, the thirty-one coloring pages make the idea of taking tea irresistible! Iced or hot—perhaps accompanied by tasty sandwiches or pastries—this refreshing beverage is represented in the most appealing way possible. Just select your media and experiment with the colors of your choice as you enjoy the artistic possibilities of this special collection—plus, the perforated, unbacked pages make displaying your work easy!

Copyright

Copyright © 2018 by Marty Noble
All rights reserved.

Bibliographical Note

Tea Time Coloring Book is a new work, first published by Dover Publications, Inc., in 2018.

International Standard Book Number

ISBN-13: 978-0-486-81746-0
ISBN-10: 0-486-81746-6

Manufactured in the United States by LSC Communications
81746602   2018
www.doverpublications.com

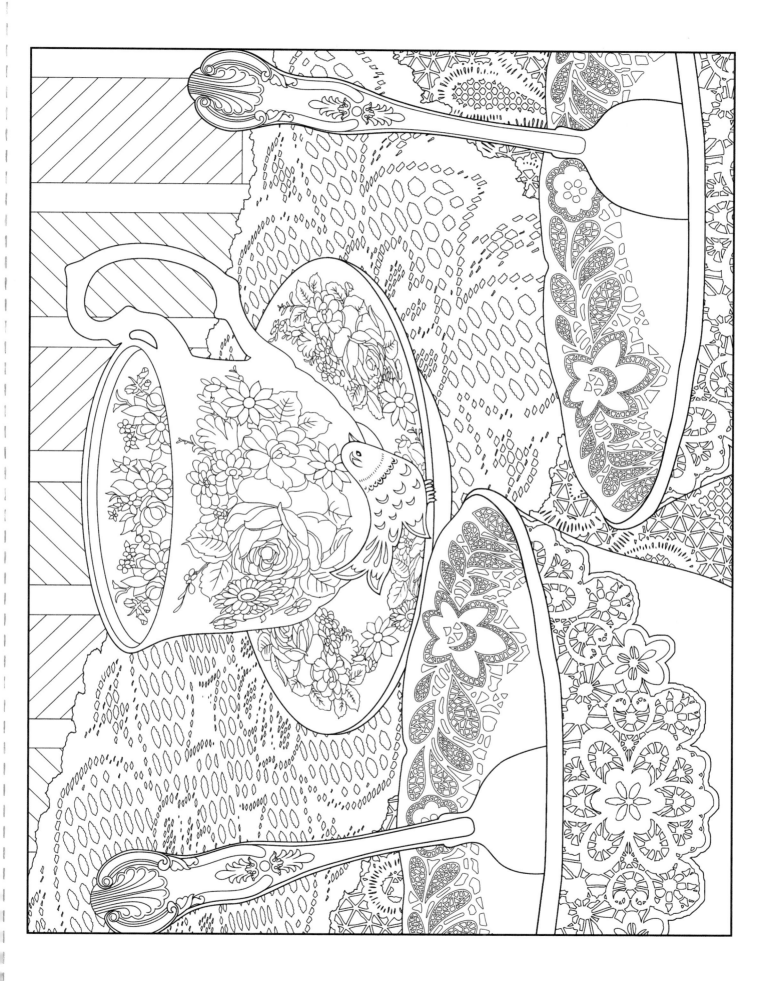

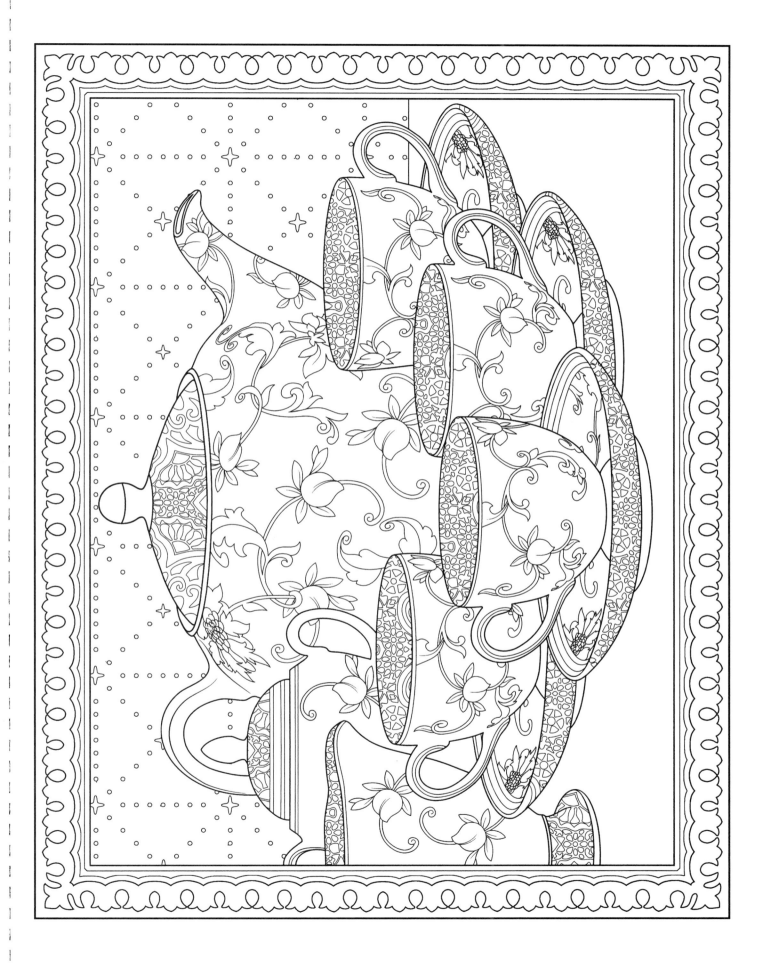